ideals
EASTER

W9-AVQ-962

It is Easter. A soft, warm breeze replaces the icy blasts of winter; the smell of rich damp earth warmed by the sun fills the air; young tender buds appear on trees that yesterday seemed barren, and tiny crocuses lift their lovely heads to the sun. The earth is responding to the touch of spring and giving of its beautiful gifts to delight the heart of man. Just as spring awakens the earth and stirs it to activity, Easter awakens the soul of man and arouses in him a divine restlessness, a desire to share his inner spiritual joy with others. It is small wonder that his heart is filled with a desire to give the message of Christ to others.

Author Unknown

Publisher, James A. Kuse
Managing Editor, Ralph Luedtke
Editor/Ideals, Colleen Callahan Gonring
Associate Editor, Linda Robinson
Production Manager, Mark Brunner
Photographic Editor, Gerald Koser
Copy Editor, Norma Barnes
Art Editor, Duane Weaver

ISBN 0-8249-1001-X 350

IDEALS—Vol. 38, No. 2 February MCMLXXXI. IDEALS (ISSN 0019-137X) is published eight times a year,
January, February, April, June, July, September, October, November
by IDEALS PUBLISHING CORPORATION, 11315 Watertown Plank Road, Milwaukee, Wis. 53226
Second class postage paid at Milwaukee, Wisconsin. Copyright © MCMLXXXI by IDEALS PUBLISHING CORPORATION.
Postmaster, please send form 3579 to Ideals Publishing Corporation, Post Office Box 2100, Milwaukee, Wis. 53201
All rights reserved. Title IDEALS registered U.S. Patent Office.
Published simultaneously in Canada.

ONE-YEAR SUBSCRIPTION—eight consecutive issues as published—$15.95
TWO-YEAR SUBSCRIPTION—sixteen consecutive issues as published—$27.95
SINGLE ISSUES—$3.50

Blossomtide

It is blossomtide again.
In the sunshine and the rain,
Thrushes sing a madrigal
For the happy festival.

From the bare bough there has come
Milk-white bloom of pear and plum.
And upon the apple tree,
Pink buds cluster daintily.

Spring's green banners are unfurled.
Joy comes back into the world.
Man may weep, but with one voice,
Nature says, "Rejoice, rejoice!"

Patience Strong

Spring Housecleaning: Toil and Drudgery

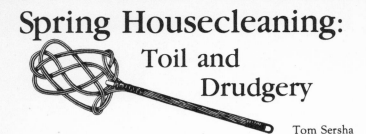

Tom Sersha

With the melting of winter's blanket of snow and the arrival of spring's warm, sunny days, most people are awakened from the winter doldrums and rejuvenated by the sounds, smells, and freshness of the spring season. Unfortunately, the housekeeper around the turn of the century had mixed feelings about spring; her pleasant thoughts were somewhat overshadowed by the toil and drudgery long associated with the annual task of "spring housecleaning."

What is generally understood as "regular spring housecleaning" was not a pleasant task for the ladies of the house but was absolutely necessary in any well-maintained household; and it was important that it be undertaken as soon as the weather permitted it. In the days when furnace grates and stoves were in constant use from six to seven months and gas lights were kept burning during many long winter nights, a very thorough housecleaning was essential to rid the home of coal dust, soot, and foul, stale air.

Usually, spring housecleaning was undertaken in late April or early May, after all the nasty weather of early spring storms, wind, and cold temperatures had subsided and milder weather and abundant sunshine filled the home. One of the first tasks confronting the housekeeper before she took steps toward the regular spring housecleaning was to rid the home of damaging moths. In early April the moths would start to emerge from their warm, cozy hiding places and begin their destruction of furs, blankets, and other choice garments. On a fairly warm day with stiff breezes, all articles of clothing would have been shaken, brushed, and hung on the clothesline to be beaten with a furniture whip or rug beater. When stored, the clothing was packed with either pepper, camphor, cedarstrips, sandalwood, or mothballs, wrapped in a clean piece of old linen, and placed in a tight cedar chest or trunk.

With this chore behind her, the lady of the house was now ready to tackle the different tasks associated with regular spring housecleaning. The wise, organized person would have planned each chore well in advance and progress in a logical manner, while maintaining order and keeping the house in habitable condition. Where did the cleaning start? It was best to commence with the cellar before any other cleaning was attempted. While cleaning the furnace and coal bin it was expected that ashes and soot would penetrate every corner of the house through the heating ducts, and the smart cleaner could attend to other areas of the house after the dust from the cellar had settled. Yes, it was the responsibility of the housekeeper to go down to the dark, dingy cellar to put the coal bin in order, remove the ashes from the furnace, scrub down the walls and floor, and brush the cobwebs away.

After the cellar was in order, work progressed to the other areas of the house, and the housekeeper must certainly have been relieved to get out of the cellar and up into the warm sunny rooms. The parlor was meticulously cared for and very clean, due to the fact that it was probably off limits to the children and their exploits. However, during spring housecleaning no corner, rug, lamp, or table was overlooked, and the room was completely stripped. The small carpets and rugs were hung on the line and beaten, on one side and then the other, with carpet beaters that ranged in size from 24 inches to 36 inches long. These beaters were made from rattan, copper wire, or galvanized wire. While holding onto the sturdy handle, most ladies may well have taken out all their cleaning frustrations and tension on the helpless rugs. Large area carpets were probably cleaned with one of several different kinds of carpet sweepers or vacuum cleaners. The Bissell's "Grand Rapids" sweeper was the best known and most widely sold carpet sweeper in the world by the turn of the century. An 1897 Sears Roebuck catalog advertisement fully describes the fine qualities found in one of their better models:

. . . Contains the famous Bissell broom action, and every other patented feature necessary in a first-class sweeper. Made from the best selected cabinet woods in an assortment of attractive finishes. Has rubber furniture protector encircling the case. Bissell's patented reversible bail spring, wheels outside the case, our everlasting pure bristle brush, both pans open at once by an easy pressure of the finger.

Vacuum cleaners were just beginning to be manufactured at this time, and from the looks of them it was probably much easier and faster to use the parlor broom. It is interesting to note that there were special parlor brooms made with the best quality corn bristles and varnished striped handles.

Most of the vacuum cleaners utilized a pump action to pick up the dirt. One such model, manufactured around 1911 and called the National Pump Action Vacuum Cleaner, was a green cylinder with a nozzle on one end and a handle on the top that was pulled up and down to create suction. It wasn't the most effective cleaner, but the colorful eagle decal made it quite attractive and prestigious. Another model, manufactured in Madison, Wisconsin, by the Wizard Manufacturing Co., resembled a small tank mounted to a wood base. A handle on one end was pumped back and forth, creating suction to draw the dirt into the hose and up to the tank. Quite primitive in comparison to our modern vacuum cleaners, these cleaners were a step in the right direction towards improving the technology that would eventually make housekeeping less strenuous for the housekeeper.

Stains on the carpets and furniture were cleaned with products found in the kitchen. Damp tea leaves or wet Indian meal was spread about the carpet and rubbed over with a broom. The curtains, ottomans, and sofas covered in worsted were cleaned with wheat bran rubbed on with flannel. It is difficult to determine how effective these home-made cleansers were, but at least they didn't cost much and the ingredients could be found in almost every home. Varnished furniture was rubbed with silk after a little sweet oil was poured over the surface. For unvarnished furniture, beeswax softened with sweet oil was applied and then polished with wool and silk rags.

The feather duster was used throughout the house to give a thorough dusting to all woodwork, walls, gas brackets, and fixtures. After the dusting, the walls and ceilings were washed, care being taken when drying that they were wiped in straight lines to avoid circles or a streaked untidy appearance. At this time it was also determined whether any painting had to be done. The chimneys and shades from the chandeliers and gas burners were washed, dried with a chamois cloth, and polished with a soft linen towel. The plated door handles, bellpulls, and other hardware were next in line for cleaning. A piece of oilcloth was cut to slip over each, so that the walls wouldn't get soiled. Hot suds and ammonia proved very effective for this work.

The proper care of the kitchen was considered by most women the foundation of all good housekeeping. Mothers who wished their daughters to grow up with the necessary domestic habits had to have, as one means of securing this result, a neat and cheerful kitchen. In the spring the walls were scrubbed and whitewashed to maintain the fresh, clean appearance. Because the range burned coal and wood, the fire box and flues accumulated thick layers of soot that had to be cleaned. Even though this chore should have been done regularly throughout the year, it was given extra special attention after the long winter.

Chambers and bedrooms were areas of the house that had to be diligently attended to if health and comfort were to be maintained in the family. Sunshine and fresh air were considered essential for good health and pleasant, cheerful homes, and the windows in these rooms were opened wide to let in the warm spring breezes and invigorating sunshine. Quilts, bed linen, and pillows were hung on the line and the mattresses were dragged outside to bask in the sun.

When the whole house had been meticulously cleaned and scoured, the housekeeper, with bowed back, aching arms, and tired feet, must have had a good feeling. A faint smile across her face and a sense of personal satisfaction inside, she knew that she had just fulfilled a very important function out of duty and love for her family and now it was her turn to look toward the beautiful spring season.

Presence

Somehow I feel God's presence here,
In a garden sprinkled with the dew;
Among the waving tulip cups,
Where miracles of spring are new.

I see Him in each petal face—
In every flower nodding there,
In roses with their sweet perfume
Wafting on the springtime air.

I find Him in the quiet place,
In green spears pushing through the sod;
And in the silence I can feel
And hear the gentle voice of God.

Angie Davidson Bass

The Touch of God

To sift the soft soil through your fingers,
To plant the small seeds one by one,
To watch each day for tiny seedlings,
To feel dependent on the sun,
To see plants grow from sprouts to flowers,
To watch them don their rainbow dress
Just makes you know God loves a garden,
For each one shows His fond caress.

Marcy Spicer

March
Symphony

Now come the first glad tidings of the spring:
    Blithe robin redbreast and his Quaker mate.
    Perched on the leafless maple by the gate,
      They give their brief, staccato twittering.

While on the mossy barn roof, pigeons coo
In tones as soft as velvet—every one—
And preen their feathers in the pale gold sun.
    Small, gray-brown sparrows scold with much ado.

      Young lambs are bleating; restless cattle low;
        Tired of the barn lot, they long for fields of green.
      The cock flings out his challenging shrill crow;
        Geese hiss at passersby with spiteful mien.

Upon the harp of winds, March ever plays
A homely tune that hints of summer days.

May Allread Baker

Spring

Rising from long winter's bed,
The crocus lifts its restless head.
It bids the tulips, "Gently rise
And shake the slumber from your eyes."
Then all the flowers, one by one,
Awaken to the warming sun.

The once-loud roar—now gentle breeze—
Of old March wind, greets budding trees.
The seeds for harvest are planted now
In beds made soft by the farmer's plow.
Wild dandelion in bright array
Spread o'er the fields a large bouquet.

The beaded drops of April's rain
Dance gingerly down my windowpane.
While droplets quench the thirsty earth
Giving field and farm an added worth.
These all tell me but one thing:
Nature has given birth to spring.

James A. Lewinski

The Magic of Spring

Spring comes dancing over the hills,
Touching her wand to the daffodils,

Causing the tulips to lift their bright heads
And rousing the violets from their mossy beds,

Exhorting the birds to burst into song
And coaxing the apple blossoms along,

Hanging the moon in the sycamore trees,
Serenading the world with sweet melodies.

And each time she comes, there is a rebirth
Of love, hope and faith upon this old earth.

Mary Ellen Stelling

The Time of the Trilliums

Colleen Reece

The haunting fragrance of years gone by reached out from the handful of wild trilliums tucked in the beautiful altar arrangement. Tearing homesickness rose within me, a longing to go back to the happy childhood I'd known, back to the time of the trilliums. The experience was not new. In all the years since I'd been a child, never did I see a trillium that I didn't remember. . . .

We lived in the country, poor in "things," rich in life itself. When the frozen earth began to thaw, when the snow had melted except in the deepest woods, when we thought we could wait no longer, we knew it was almost time. Then on some certain Saturday morning Mom would hang up her apron, Dad would lay aside his axe, and all the chores needing to be done. They would call my brothers and me for our annual family expedition. It was the time of the trilliums.

It was usually sunny, but cold in the shady spots. We climbed over, or under, or through our barbed wire fence, (depending on who we were) and followed the faint path that in summer became more well defined, until we came to "The Hill" back of our place and above the river. "The Hill" was only one of many, yet for us it was special—it was ours. Close enough to the back fence to hear Mom call, yet far enough away to be deliciously adventurous, we bicycled, walked, or slid on it, depending on the season. But now we only went to the top and sides. That's where the object of our search would be.

The woods were carpeted with flowers. Wild bleeding hearts, tiny yellow "Johnny jump-ups," even smaller purple wood violets—and wild trilliums (we called them "Easter lilies" then). They grew by the hundreds, but we picked only those we'd be using. In later years, we'd heard, they won't continue to bloom well if picked; so our outing was made with buckets and shovels, and in time the giant fir trees in our yard were encircled with the indescribable beauty of those wild white flowers.

Our family was a complete unit on those tramps, untouched by the outside world, calling to one another to "come see!" the blinking toad, the

in the winter snows, coming to life again when God smiled warmly in the springtime? Had we not seen for ourselves the stark tree branches etched against the stormy sky, which began to swell and burst with buds and shoots of green when God wept over His mistreated Son and caused the spring rains to fall as Easter approached? No one had to convince us there was a Resurrection of the dead. We saw it every year, and we knew it was true.

There were other walks, and jaunts, and trips. Summer found us armed with fish poles, fry pans, and potatoes on the banks of river and stream at the end of a hard day's work. The red-gold world of Autumn called us leaf hunting, November storms were to be followed with a walk to the river and stream to see how their courses had been changed by the wild beatings. We watched our old friends, the happy creek and river, roaring and crowding their banks, no longer the companions we loved in summer, but strangers, fulfilling their purpose in rushing to the sea. We carried home driftwood from their shores for the wood stoves and the cold days to come. With February came the warm, moist "chinook wind," with a feeling and smell like no other wind on earth. It heralded the snow water runoff from the hills, again flooding the frozen creeks and ponds, and we knew the time of the trilliums was almost with us again.

What was it that made that first spring outing so cherished? Was it the welcome release from scratchy winter clothes—the freedom from cold—the rareness of our folks dropping all their Saturday work to be with us—the beauty of a fresh-washed world? Or was it the togetherness, those loving memories tying us together and to God and His creation with invisible threads neither time nor distance can break? I cannot say, I do not know.

The years have passed, bringing increase, taking their toll. Mom's hair is snow-white now; there are great-grandchildren following her to the cookie jar. My brothers and I are getting gray, a little tired, a little slower. Dad was the first to start down the "unknown trail"—leading the way, breaking the path as he did so many times before. We miss him, yet have no fear. He's just a few steps ahead, around a shady bend, a little out of sight. Many times I feel very close to him, and wonder just how long it will be until we all catch up—but never so strongly as in the time of the trilliums.

chattering squirrel, the pheasant, or the robin, rabbit, and any other treasure denied us during the long, hard winters. They were times of discovery, of learning, of love. Mom had been a teacher, Dad was a woodsman, and our outdoors classroom was infinitely more appealing than regular school. Perhaps our first appreciation of God's love to the world was learned there in His handiwork and beauty.

As we grew, so did our understanding. We had no trouble accepting the great truths of life, such as Creation or the Resurrection. Had we not seen the ugly dead bulbs and vines lying about, to be buried

Serenity

Here, where the April gypsy breezes pass,
Swaying the spring-lit lanterns on each tree
That arches above the newly wakened grass,
I gaze with awesome breath at all I see:

A silken foal,
White lambs along the fence,
Trilliums that grow
In bright exuberance,
Nodding in rhythm
With the songs that spill
From post to post,
As winging birds fulfill
A green-framed vista
Of infinity—
This day, a part
Of all eternity.

Kneeling to touch a white, tri-petaled bell
I feel God's presence, know all will be well.
A tender feeling stirs within my breast,
A sense of peace, of gratefulness, and rest.

Eleanor Pautz

Talk with a Little Girl

My little girl, may there
Never come an hour
You can pass by, indifferent,
A first spring flower.

Or never miss the magic music
Of a gentle little bird,
To linger for a lifetime
Long after it is heard.

Or the mystery of starshine,
With its everlasting light,
To hold you captive in its spell
On some far starless night.

My little girl, may there
Never come a day
You do not have the eyes to see
All beauty on your way.

Lucille Crumley

Spring Comes

Edna Jaques

Spring has such gracious hands! She brings
   The essence of all lovely things,
New petaled gorse, the flame of broom,
   Warm sunlight in a quiet room,
Small leaves unfolding every hour,
   The still, sweet opening of a flower.

Spring has such lovely hands! She yields
   Her warmth and beauty to the fields,
Wooing the Earth with wind and rain,
   Clothing the hills with green again.
New lambs with wee, unsteady feet,
   New grass in pastures warm and sweet.

Spring has such willing hands! She weaves
   Her magic tapestry of leaves,
Like a thatched roof above my head,
   And for my feet a carpet spread
With woof of scarlet, warp of brown,
   Woven of moss as soft as down.

Spring is the quickening, the birth,
   The resurrection of the earth.
There is no death of anything.
   Life walks triumphant through the spring,
Trailing her glory like a cloak
   Above the heads of common folk.

The Child Jesus

He played, a child like you or me,
   In fields and streets of Galilee.
He laughed and shouted merrily.
   He fished the stream and climbed the tree.

He worked at learning Joseph's trade
   With hammer, saw, and planing blade.
As Joseph showed him, he obeyed,
   And useful things in wood he made.

Then studied, after work and play,
   To grow in wisdom in God's way,
And went upon the Sabbath Day
   Unto the synagogue to pray.

His hair sun-bleached, his face sun-tanned;
   In sleeveless tunic Mary's hand
Had woven; at waist, a linen band;
   His feet in sandals, see him stand.

Dorothy Russell

Thou Art a Teacher Come from God

Although we are not told anything in the Gospels about the schooling of Jesus, the writer of Luke said that the boy "increased in wisdom." Since early Hebrews wanted their sons to read the Scriptures, it is likely that Joseph sent Jesus to the local synagogue school to learn to read. What kind of a school was it?

According to old records, the first elementary school in the Holy Land opened about seventy-five years before Jesus was born. It was started by a queen and her brother who was a rabbi. Perhaps he became the first grammar school teacher.

Gradually small towns about the land copied the example of Jerusalem and opened a House of the Books. This was not a separate building, but was the synagogue. Here classes were held on weekdays and worship on the Sabbath.

The most important building in every village was the synagogue. It was placed on the highest piece of ground as a symbol that it was sacred. It also faced toward the Holy City.

The building had only one room. Because wood was both scarce and costly, the walls were made from the stones that littered the land. The floor was paved with flat stones. Along the sides of the walls were stone benches for the males who came to worship. Set into one wall was a special bench known as the Moses seat. This was for the school teacher on weekdays.

The walls held no pictures of famous men, not even of the prophets. Drawings of humans were considered to be related to idolatry. However, a local artist might have painted palms over the stones. This was permitted because palms decorated Solomon's Temple (1 Kings 6:29). There might also have been a six-pointed or five-pointed star.

The main furnishing in the room was a chest or ark placed on the east wall. This was a symbol of the Holy of Holies in the great Temple. Inside the ark was a scroll of the Law, the sacred Torah. And in front of the ark a lamp burned day and night, year in and year out, a token of everlasting Truth.

On nearby shelves rested more scrolls of Scrip-ture to be used as textbooks for the pupils. Each scroll was in a leather case wrapped in linen. In one corner of the room stood the shophar, a horn that was blown to announce the start of the Sabbath at Friday sunset. The horn was a ram's horn which had been straightened by heat and flattened at one end.

Each synagogue had a lectern where the speaker stood to read. At his elbow a set of seven candles, the menorah, threw light on the written words.

The school teacher was a rabbi, if one was available in the town. If not, then a scholar gave his time to the classroom and was paid by the congregation. A rabbi, however, was not so lucky. Although he had spent months or years earning his title at a rabbinical college, he received no salary. Instead, he was expected to support himself by a trade working with his hands.

Students in the classroom were boys. Though there was no law forbidding a girl to go to school, the men had decided that reading and writing were not necessary for a female. Her place in life would always be in a home, since there were no lady scribes, secretaries, lawyers or rulers of the synagogue.

Segregation was unheard of. The color of skin was of no importance. Some boys had very dark complexions because they had a dark ancestor named Ham. Other students had light complexions and looked almost Greek. Their ancestor had been Japheth, third son of Noah.

Jesus may have gone to this type of school. We have no record that He ever taught school, yet He became a teacher. The Gospels report that He "went about all Galilee, teaching in their synagogues" (Matt. 4:23). Possibly He had even studied in a rabbinical college, since He was addressed by the title of rabbi. A judge of the Hebrew supreme court, the Sanhedrin, saluted Jesus as, "Rabbi, we know thou art a teacher come from God" (John 3:2).

Yet this greatest of all men may have started in a little schoolhouse in a synagogue in Nazareth.

Helen B. Walters

Desert in Spring

Margaret Turner Porter

Today I walked in God's backyard,
  Through endless fields of flowers,
That stretched in all directions toward
  His mountain palace towers.

The ground was softly carpeted
  With buttercups of gold,
With lupines blue and clover red,
  And purple thistles bold.

As God pulled down the shades of night,
  Winds warmed by desert heat
Brought rare perfume that filled the air
  With scented sagebrush sweet.

Grotesquely stood the Joshua trees
  As though in expectation,
Like gnarled and twisted hands outstretched
  In silent supplication.

From out the dusk there came the strains
  Of music sweet, as though
The wind and trees in harmony
  Were singing soft and low.

Perhaps the breeze was angels' harps
  That floated through the sky;
Those groping fingers were upreached
  To play as they passed by.

Oberammergau: A Special Balm for the Traveler's Soul

The highway southwest from Munich scoots across the south German countryside like a slightly bent arrow. The road crunches into the foothills of the Bavarian Alps and reels off to the dancing tune of the wind-carved crags. No longer straight, but with enough switchbacks and curves to keep one's vehicle on a seemingly perpetual tilt, the road makes its way toward the Austrian border.

The crests stand in review on either side, towering over the valleys that tiptoe among the rocks. The peaks—Laberjoch, Notkarspitze, Zahn, Kofel, Aufacker, Puerschling, Ettaler Manndl—stare down from their snow-tipped caps. Romans marched through here centuries ago, and generations of salt carts were hauled precariously along these same passes.

The armies and merchants were on their own sorts of pilgrimages during those days. Now the visitor makes his or her way into these Upper Bavarian ranges for different reasons. This is the Werdenfelser land, an untranslatable tag that has some colloquial tie-in with the great boulders and gorges.

Whatever the meaning, the beauty of this region cannot be denied. Whatever the season—from the edelweiss-freckled spring to the sparkling white of the winter horizon—the district offers a special balm for the traveler's soul. The country folk here are still fiercely religious, with their shrines dotting the edges of the walking paths, the bulbous-domed churches sprouting like holy mushrooms in the fields and enough processions to celebrate almost every major feast on the church calendar.

It is a land steeped in the customs of a simpler age, when faith meant everything. Yet, it is a land where one can live harmoniously alongside the trendy jet setters, athletes and everyday tourists who frequent the health resorts and ski lodges throughout the countryside.

Amid this vibrant mingling of nature and differing lifestyle, sits Oberammergau. The village, barely more than fifty miles from sprawling Munich, perches astride one of the main roads through the mountain vastness. Because of its strategic location, Oberammergau is cosmopolitan, international and lively, yet retains, in the ornate baroque architecture throughout the town, an Old-World flavor. The spires of the Lutheran and Catholic churches in town ensure that at least the eyes, if not the total spirits, of visitors point toward the heavens.

The town of about five-thousand citizens depends primarily on tourism, followed in succession by an extensive woodcarving and pottery industry, shops and farming. Some 250 master carvers live in the area, each offering a personalized "handgeschnitzt," or guaranteed seal of craftsmanship on the pieces they produce. Primarily religious in theme, the carvers' work finds its way around the world.

But what truly sets Oberammergau apart from its just-as-lovely and tourist-conscious neighbors, is its commitment to a generations-old tradition. Mention the village name and immediately the Oberammergau Passion Play comes to mind. The play has been performed nearly every decade since the misery-ridden Middle Ages when plague and warfare ravaged all of Europe.

In 1633, when sickness snatched away most of the inhabitants of the village, the parish priests desperately promised that they would stage a performance of the Passion of Christ every ten years if the plague departed. The story says that, from that moment, the community was spared further horror.

Continued

The inhabitants fulfilled their oath, and their descendants have followed suit. The 1980 presentation was the thirty-seventh production of the Passion in Oberammergau. Although the play usually has been presented every decade, a performance was given in 1934 on the 300th anniversary of the play and a special production is being considered for 1984, the 350th anniversary.

The text of the play was rewritten between 1850 and 1860 by Fr. Alois Daisenberger, an Oberammergau priest. The form was retained fairly intact until the 1970 and 1980 productions, when slight revisions were introduced. The music for the Passion Play was composed in 1815 by Rochus Dedler, a local school teacher, and his work has continued to be the backbone of the choral and orchestral arrangements. Such local involvement has always been obvious, with town residents taking a strong part in behind-the-scenes activity as well as on-stage work.

For years, even before the hirsute hippie look became popular, Oberammergau males were easily identified by their beards and long hair — kept in readiness for the next production. Just about everyone in town has a story to tell about the time (or times) he or she participated in the Passion Play. The record has been held by 81-year-old Melchior Breitsamter, who debuted on stage at age six and subsequently performed in nine of the plays. He took the role of Pontius Pilate in 1930, 1934, 1950 and 1960 and the role of Annas in 1980.

A special town council meeting elects the major performers a year prior to the show, and a look through the archives of the play shows that the same family names crop up each decade. More than a thousand town citizens are involved in the performances, and all must remain amateurs. If a player or musician connected with the production strikes out for the bright theatrical lights elsewhere, he or she cannot again appear in the performance. Traditionally, female participation is limited to single residents of thirty-five years or younger.

The play depicts the story of Christ's Passion beginning with the entry into Jerusalem and ending with the Resurrection and Transfiguration. A performance lasts an entire day, opening at 9 A.M. and concluding about 4:30 P.M., with a two-hour midday lunch break. The performance is given only in German, but English, French, Swedish and Danish texts are available for theatergoers.

The immense open-air stage can accommodate 800 performers at one time, with a covered auditorium seating 5,200 persons. Fourteen gates allow everyone to leave at the end of the show within five minutes, in true Germanic precision. Nearly 500,000 persons see the shows, out of two million requests, at the 102 performances that are usually staged during the summer in which the play is presented.

When not hosting the Passion Play production, the massive building is often used for international music festivals and concerts by touring companies. The Mormon Tabernacle Choir and numerous other American groups have presented programs on the Oberammergau stage.

A nearby Passion Play museum contains numerous artifacts dating back to the earliest presentations. Included are a 300-year-old table that was used for the Last Supper scene; 200-year-old costumes made by monks in the nearby monastery at Ettal; papier-mache dioramas of religious scenes; and an old Christmas creche containing 120 human and 80 animal figures handmade by local carvers.

Even standing outside the empty auditorium, one can feel the atmosphere of love and faith that caused all this to come about. The entire town is a living monument to that dedication, that yearning to be something beyond itself—to fulfill a promise made 300 years ago.

During the show's prologue, an actor sonorously proclaims to the audience, "Look . . . not for the faults of others in this story, but recognize your own guilt . . . "

In whatever language, the fervor of the Oberammergau Passion Play gives all of us that living message.

Martin Hintz

Easter Flowers

Easter, so beautiful! Glorious,
 skies seem forever blue,
As all nature, revived and pulsating,
 bursts forth anew,
Symbolizing, through each tiny seed
 rising up from the sod,
The glorious Resurrection of Christ,
 the Son of God.
Eastertime means life anew, and we,
 just like the flowers,
Redeemed shall rise from the dust.
 Eternal life is ours.

Eva Adams

Triumph

Up and down, o'er hill and valley,
 Sounds the Easter jubilee.
Breezes sing it, echoes fling it—
 Bursting bud, and leaf, and tree—
Whispers of the life to be.

All the world is full of glory;
 All the bonds of death are riven.
Listen to the swelling chorus:
 Christ, the Lord, has risen! Risen!

Sing, O earth. Fling wide the story,
 While the echoes ring, and ring,
Pulsing, throbbing, with the glory:
 Grave is conquered! Christ is King!

L. D. Stearns

The Last Supper

Now when the even was come, he sat down with the twelve. And as they did eat, he said, "Verily I say unto you, that one of you shall betray me." And they were exceeding sorrowful, and began every one of them to say unto him, "Lord, is it I?" And he answered and said, "He that dippeth his hand with me in the dish, the same shall betray me. The Son of man goeth as it is written of him; but woe unto that man by whom the Son of man is betrayed! It had been good for that man if he had not been born." Then Judas, which betrayed him, answered and said, "Master, is it I?" He said unto him, "Thou hast said."

And as they were eating, Jesus took bread, and blessed it, and brake it, and gave it to the disciples, and said, "Take, eat; this is my body." And he took the cup, and gave thanks, and gave it to them, saying, "Drink ye all of it, for this is my blood of the new testament, which is shed for many for the remission of sins. But I say unto you, I will not drink henceforth of this fruit of the vine, until that day when I drink it new with you in my Father's kingdom."

Matthew 26:20-29

The Sleeping Disciples

Then cometh Jesus with them unto a place called Gethsemane, and saith unto the disciples, "Sit ye here, while I go and pray yonder." And he took with him Peter and the two sons of Zebedee, and began to be sorrowful and very heavy. Then saith he unto them, "My soul is exceeding sorrowful, even unto death: tarry ye here, and watch with me."

And he went a little farther, and fell on his face, and prayed, saying, "O my Father, if it be possible, let this cup pass from me: nevertheless not as I will, but as thou wilt." And he cometh unto the disciples, and findeth them asleep, and saith unto Peter, "What, could ye not watch with me one hour? Watch and pray, that ye enter not into temptation: the spirit indeed is willing, but the flesh is weak."

He went away again the second time, and prayed, saying, "O my Father, if this cup may not pass away from me, except I drink it, thy will be done." And he came and found them asleep again, for their eyes were heavy. And he left them, and went away again, and prayed the third time, saying the same words.

Then cometh he to his disciples, and saith unto them, "Sleep on now, and take your rest; behold, the hour is at hand, and the Son of man is betrayed into the hands of sinners. Rise, let us be going; behold, he is at hand that doth betray me."

Matthew 26:36-46

As winter snows receded and the sun rose higher each day to herald the coming spring, peasant women of the Ukraine prepared to celebrate the Resurrection with an art far older than Christianity.

Their symbols of spring's rebirth and fertility were tiny, vivid masterpieces—geometric patterns of flowers, animals, intricate cross-hatchings and complex borders, all full of ancient meaning and glowing with the colors of natural dyes.

And the "canvas" upon which the peasant women worked was the most fragile and delicate imaginable—a new-laid hen's egg.

Ukrainian Easter eggs, once limited to the steppes and forests of southwestern Russia and produced in patterns handed down from mother to daughter for centuries, are today recognized as treasures of folk art. Private collections and museums cherish outstanding examples of *pysanky*— "written eggs"—some specimens being fifty or eighty years old. And the creation of pysanky has spread far beyond the Ukraine, as emigrants and their descendants, and modern craftspeople as well, have revived the ancient art.

Technically, the creation of Ukrainian Easter eggs is fairly simple, rather like batik, in which lines of melted beeswax shield parts of a design from repeated dye-baths. But spiritually and esthetically, far more has been involved.

In the beginning, the egg itself was deeply significant. To the pagans of old it symbolized the primeval world-egg, from which all creation was hatched. Broken open, it revealed the yellow yolk, like the brilliant sun-god who was reborn each spring to rescue the world from the dark grip of winter. And, like the quickening earth, the egg could mysteriously bring forth new life. Small wonder that it was venerated and became the basis for a sacred art, replete with powerful symbols.

After Christianity came to the Ukraine, those ancient symbols were converted to Christian meanings—and the creation of pysanky continued, with the blessing of the church, as a ritual of Easter.

The forty days before Easter were a time of spiritual cleansing for Ukrainians. Disputes were resolved and forgiven, and old friendships renewed.

After the rest of the family were asleep, the women of a household would gather for their annual making of pysanky. Having spent the day peacefully, avoiding gossip and dealing lovingly with the family, each woman was thus placed in a proper spiritual state. She would murmur a short prayer, "God help and guide us," and begin.

Taking a fresh, whole egg in one hand and a *kistka,* a tiny metal cone wired to a wooden handle, in the other, the woman would fill the kistka with a tiny dollop of beeswax and then heat it in the flame of a candle. Then, through the hollow point of the cone, the melted wax, now blackened with candle soot, was drawn onto the surface of the egg in sure, steady strokes, following patterns which had evolved over centuries. First the egg was divided according to one of twelve traditional "divisions," then each segment was subdivided according to the artist's inclination and skill. As she worked, the woman would sing softly, to soothe the wandering souls—*dukhe*—which inhabited the night.

After each layer of wax-lines covered part of the design, the egg was dipped in a different colored dye. Derived from local plants, the natural dyes were, like the patterns, passed down in certain villages, sometimes even in single families.

Old-World Easter

White, the color of purity and innocence, was created by covering large areas of the design with wax. After the eggs were dipped in yellow, symbolic of increase, another layer of wax lines preserved the color's part in the pattern; then came the green of spring or the blue of health, followed by the red of the sun, and the black of the darkest part of the night. After this final bath the egg was completely covered with hardened, soot-black beeswax. This was carefully softened alongside the candle flame, and wiped away with a cloth—and, magically, the intricate, rainbow-hued egg emerged from the somber darkness that had concealed it.

After coating with varnish to protect the design and seal the pores of the shell, the egg was set aside to dry. Over time, the interior of the egg would desiccate and harden into a dry lump; sealed eggs do not spoil. The finished pysanka was then ready for use.

While modern collectors and craftspeople enjoy the beauty of these eggs, in the Ukraine, and in traditional Ukrainian households in America, pysanky served many purposes.

Different blessings were invoked upon every egg. Some pysanky were intended as gifts between friends and relatives. A bowl of pysanky in the home was said to keep fire and lightning away and bring good luck and happiness.

Pysanky were tokens of love when given by a maid to a boy. A young bride was presented with a pysanka decorated with the image of a hen, ancient symbol of fertility; if no children were forthcoming, her husband was then presented a pysanka decorated with a rooster. Children were given eggs decorated with flowers, and incorporating large areas of the white of innocence; old people were given pysanky in darker colors, decorated with the gates and ladders which symbolize the transition to another world.

The farmer buried special pysanky in his fields, or fed his farm animals decorated eggs to increase their fertility; eggs were hung in barns to protect them, and buried beneath the foundations of a new house. Everywhere, pysanky were designed to repel evil and strengthen goodness. Symbols, colors, prayers, and blessings by the village priest all gave added power to the Easter eggs.

Every spring, the old Ukrainians said, the Evil One traveled the world to see how many pysanky had been made that year. If few were to be found, he was encouraged to extend his dark dominion; if many were visible, he withdrew in fear. The ancient spiral pattern, dating far back into prehistory, was a particularly effective trap for wandering demons. Attracted to the inward-turning design, they were imprisoned forever at its center.

The most powerful and sacred of the old symbols was, of course, the sun—originally representing the sun-god, later Christ. Birds represented spring, rebirth, good fortune. Stags or goats invoked wealth. Triangles stood for the Trinity. Circles and meanders represented supernatural protection and everlasting life. All these, with many others, are still incorporated into the tiny, brilliant works of art created by the women of the Ukraine—to be given and treasured as symbols of the annual miracle of rebirth, and of the strong bonds between the Ukrainian people and their ancient heritage.

Walter J. Wentz

Christ in Bondage

And so Pilate, willing to content the people, released Barabbas unto them, and delivered Jesus, when he had scourged him, to be crucified.

And the soldiers led him away into the hall, called Praetorium; and they called together the whole band. And they clothed him with purple, and platted a crown of thorns, and put it about his head, and began to salute him, "Hail, King of the Jews!" And they smote him on the head with a reed, and did spit upon him, and bowing their knees worshipped him. And when they had mocked him, they took off the purple from him, and put his own clothes on him, and led him out to crucify him.

Mark 15:15-20

My Son—My Savior

Dorothy Doutt Minchew

So much has happened in only a few days. The stately green palm branches that were strewn as a path for the "King" are now brown from the sun and bruised and torn almost beyond recognition from the feet of countless visitors. Thousands have streamed into Jerusalem for this most festive of religious occasions—this festive occasion that is turning into a nightmare.

My son has been betrayed by one of his own followers. Sold! For thirty pieces of silver! Because it is "expedient that one should die," Jesus has been turned over to Pilate to be crucified, while the thoughtless crowd shouts for the release of a common thief by the name of Barabbas. And now, by the simple act of washing his hands, Pilate becomes another of those whose hideous insults Jesus must bear.

I cannot stand much more of this anguish. I have no more tears. The hot ache in my parched throat makes it impossible for me to speak. As I stand helplessly by and watch my son being so cruelly mistreated by men, women, and children who are not worthy even to be in his presence, I wish that he had not even been born. He has tried so valiantly to do his heavenly Father's bidding, and it has been such a difficult task. Why has so much been demanded from him?

Surely God, in His great wisdom, could have found another answer to man's sin.

"Blessed art thou among women."

Those words echo in my ears. Blessed? Blessed to know that from my womb has come one who will suffer an agony so horrible that even God must surely blacken all the earth to keep from seeing it?

Oh, God, did You forget? Do You not know, above all others, what pain a mother's heart contains? Is it only the one who nurtures her babe that aches as her son aches?

My baby son! How happy Joseph and I were when you were born that star-filled night in Bethlehem! You were such a tiny bundle of joy for both of us. As the angels heralded your birth, we knew that you were someone special.

My pain is almost unbearable, watching the soldiers mock you, as they dress you in a scarlet robe and press a crown of thorns upon your brow.

Where now, my son, are your faithful followers—even Peter?

Oh! I have been pushed down by the rushing mob and cannot even get a glimpse of him! As I lie here, unable to rise, I cannot help thinking back to his twelfth year, when Joseph and I brought him to Jerusalem for the Passover. How different it was from this day! Little did we realize that that year was the turning point in his life—until we discovered that he had not followed us as we left. When we returned to find him, we were amazed to hear him speaking with such wisdom and authority in the midst of learned men. Suddenly, I realized that my son surely was no ordinary boy.

It was from that day that I began to know that he belonged more to God than to me.

At last, I can rise to my feet and see Jesus again. They have now clothed him in his own garments.

Be strong, Son! Stop there and rest! He is on his way up the Hill of Golgotha, laboring under the weight of the cumbrous cross. Splinters from the roughhewn wood have pierced his hands and streams of blood pour forth from the swollen purple bruises.

Oh, God, I cannot bear it any longer!

There are more tears! I thought there were none left. But God, in His mercy, has granted me once more a sweet release, as hot, relentless tears rush down my burning cheeks and muffled shrieks cut into my throat.

I can only watch in dismay and disbelief as the Roman soldiers raise the crude wooden cross on which his body hangs. I want to beat upon them with my fists, but I am too weak from grief to stir. I hear his barely audible whisper, "I thirst." Dear God, have mercy on my son!

My eyes dim with tears as I think of the wedding guests whose thirst he quenched. It was in Galilee, at a great wedding feast in Cana, that I asked Jesus to perform his first miracle. He was astonished that I asked, but he did my bidding. That was the first time we shared openly what we had both known in secret.

He, whom I have seen perform miracles, cannot now even satisfy the longing on his own parched lips for a sip of cool water.

"He saved others; himself he cannot save!"

I have to clamp my trembling hands over my ears to block out the invidious jeering and shouting. Do they not care? Is it nothing to them—all those who pass by?

I did not suppose that it would come to such a time as this!

Nor do I understand how Jesus can ask for mercy for those who are committing this heinous act against him, how he can plead with God to "forgive them."

I want my son to show them all—spineless Pilate, the too-loyal Roman soldiers, the cruel mob—what special powers he possesses. But no! The torture continues hour after sickening hour as I watch the life's blood run out of him.

Oh, how faint I am. His hours on the cross seem unending. How much longer, God, before the anguish of this unholy day becomes a haunting memory?

The full power of Jesus' mission is beginning to unfold. I hear him tell the thief on the cross next to him that his sins are forgiven and that they will be together this very day in Paradise.

I was not aware that I was moving so close to the cross. But, all of a sudden, I am on John's arms, standing directly at the foot of the cross.

I look up into the eyes of my dying son. But he, in spite of his agony and suffering, sees only my grief, not his own. With a look of love, he is trying to relieve the agony which he knows is tearing at my heart.

As he asked John to take care of me, a drop of his precious blood fell from his thorn-crowned brow onto mine.

I must reach up to him.

And as I gaze into His face, I do not see my son. I see my Savior.

Now upon the first day of the week, very early in the morning, they came unto the sepulchre, bringing the spices which they had prepared, and certain others with them. And they found the stone rolled away from the sepulchre. And they entered in, and found not the body of the Lord Jesus.

And it came to pass, as they were much perplexed thereabout, behold, two men stood by them in shining garments. And as they were afraid, and bowed down their faces to the earth, they said unto them, "Why seek ye the living among the dead? He is not here, but is risen: remember how he spake unto you when he was yet in Galilee, saying, 'The Son of man must be delivered into the hands of sinful men, and be crucified, and the third day rise again.'"

And they remembered his words, and returned from the sepulchre, and told all these things unto the eleven, and to all the rest.

Luke 24:1-9

But ye shall receive power, after that the Holy Ghost is come upon you: and ye shall be witnesses unto me both in Jerusalem, and in all Judea, and in Samaria, and unto the uttermost part of the earth." And when he had spoken these things, while they beheld, he was taken up; and a cloud received him out of their sight.

And while they looked steadfastly toward heaven as he went up, behold, two men stood by them in white apparel; which also said, "Ye men of Galilee, why stand ye gazing up into heaven? This same Jesus, which is taken up from you into heaven, shall so come in like manner as ye have seen him go into heaven."

Acts 1:8-11

Consider the Lilies

Harold W. Rock

"Consider the lilies how they grow: they toil not, they spin not; and yet I say unto you, that Solomon in all his glory was not arrayed like one of these."

Luke 12:27

Although the word "lilies" probably referred to the tulip, narcissus, or the anemone, translators for the King James Bible thought it very appropriate to use the word "lilies" in this particular verse. Thereby, they gave a very deserved compliment to a worldwide family of attractive flowering plants whose blooms have been renowned for their eye-catching beauty.

Traditionally, lilies were used as symbols of the beauty of God's creation, and the white lilies were particularly favored to symbolize both beauty and purity. Since early in the history of man, they have been popular as decorations at funerals and other sacred ceremonies, and early Christian churches used white lilies widely as the festive Easter flower.

The Easter lily could be any one of a number of white lilies, including the Madonna Lily of Greece, the Formosa Lily of China, the Asiatic Regal Lily, and the Bermuda or Harris Lily from southern Japan. The one that has become the modern day Easter lily is the Bermuda Lily (*Lilium Longiflorum*) which was discovered by missionaries about 160 years ago and brought to Bermuda and England. This handsome white lily was found to be easily brought into bloom from seed within a few months and could readily be "forced" at the desired time. "Forcing" is a process often used commercially by which plants are brought to maturity, by the use of heat and special lighting, outside the normal season.

About fifty years ago, the Croft, a variety very efficient in forming offset bulbs, was developed in the United States. The ease with which it can be forced and its efficiency in forming offset bulbs have made the Croft the most desirable commercial lily for Easter decorations to this day.

Many varieties and strains of the *Lilium longiflorum* have been developed over the years, including the dwarf Creole, widely grown in the New Orlean's area, the older variety *eximium*, often called the Bermuda or Harris Lily, which has wide commercial distribution, and the newer Estate which is valuable in supplying cut flowers. These and other variations have not had the commercial appeal of the Croft.

When an Easter lily is purchased or received as a gift, it will bloom readily for a few weeks, if kept moderately watered in a cool, draft-free, well-lighted site. It can be made to bloom again if the growing conditions remain favorable. Continue to keep the plant in bright light and watered until the foliage starts to brown. Then cease watering, and allow it to dry completely in a dark place. In May, remove the bulb from the pot with roots intact, and plant it at a depth of six inches in a sunny, well-drained spot with loose, moderately-rich soil. Often, it will produce one or two flowers in late summer or early fall.

In the North, Easter lily bulbs are not winter-hardy, outdoors, but a few survive when in a sheltered, southern exposure and well mulched. In mid-America they generally survive in a sheltered area if heavily mulched and protected from early frost. In the South and Southwest they can be grown in open areas provided they, too, are protected from early frost. Many growers suggest that the bulbs be started in pots in the greenhouse or other sheltered areas and placed outdoors in late May. The plants bloom in July and August with one to six large, fragrant, pure white, trumpet-shaped flowers on two- to three-foot stems.

Another way to handle your gift Easter lily is to leave it in the pot after it has dried, placing it outdoors in May in a good growing site. Water lightly until the new shoots appear and then water freely. Fertilize every two weeks with liquids or once every month with flowerpot spikes. The plant will usually rebloom in August. The weakened bulb should then be discarded.

If you wish to force a bulb indoors, you can have moderate success even if there are not greenhouse conditions. Use a fresh, healthy bulb and plant singly in a five- or 6-inch pot at a depth of one or two inches in a standard soil mix during September, October or November. Keep in a shaded cold frame for a month if the weather is mild. When bulbs are brought indoors, keep them in bright light, preferably with a 60° F night temperature. The soil should be kept moist from the time of planting. Timing for blooms is not easy, but florists find that high temperatures speed up the opening of buds.

The beautiful Croft Easter Lily enhances the formal indoor sites of homes and edifices and the more formal areas of terraces, but frequently it is too stiff and formal and too short to fit well into more informal gardens. For such purposes, there is a large selection of beautiful, sturdy lilies that can be chosen. Limiting the choice to only the white lilies, the following are excellent selections: the ancient, lovely, easily grown Regal Lily, which is both robust and disease resistant; the large, sturdy, attractive, trumpet-shaped, white Olympic Hybrids; the more difficult to grow but beautiful *L. martagon album*, called the White European Turkscap Lily; and the lovely, nodding, white Aurelian Hybrids, including the yellow-centered Bright Star which is one of the most easily grown. The Madonna and the Formosa lilies are too subject to diseases to be included. There are so many gorgeous, multicolored hybrid lilies which are sturdy and disease resistant that plant lovers should not neglect to get acquainted with their outstanding qualities as garden flowers.

Clustered lilies in the shadows
Lapt in golden ease they stand,
Rarest flower in all the meadows
Richest flower in all the land.

    —Dora Read Goodak

The Lily's Message

Marie Elmore Baxter

The Easter lily blooms again
From out the deep, dark sod;
Its snowy bells bring messages
With every graceful nod.

The lily speaks of purity,
Of faith and trust and love;
It bids us to be grateful for
Each blessing from above.

It speaks of everlasting life
That came from out the tomb,
Upon that far-off Easter morn
When Christ cast off death's gloom.

To walk again with those He loved,
To touch the fragrant flowers
That grew within the garden walls,
To spend more happy hours

With those who had believed Him dead,
Who mourned Him as one gone,
The lily bids us greet Him now,
This blessed Easter dawn!

Easter is a joyous season, reflecting the hope of the Resurrection following the despair of the Crucifixion. The blossoming flowers and plants of springtime also convey this eternal message of hope for mankind. A number of plants which bloom during the Easter season have been specifically associated with the Passion of our Savior. A variety of fascinating myths and legends have developed over the centuries concerning certain conspicuous markings on these flowering plants.

One such legend involves our native eastern dogwood tree. Although this tree was unknown in biblical lands, it remains the focal point of one of the best-known American tree legends relating to the Crucifixion of Christ. The story goes:

"At the time of the Crucifixion, the dogwood had been the size of the oak and other forest trees. So firm and strong was the tree that it was chosen as the timber for the cross. To be used thus for such a cruel purpose greatly distressed the tree, and Jesus, nailed upon it, sensed this, and in his gentle pity for all sorrow and suffering said to it, 'Because of your regret and pity for my suffering, never again shall the dogwood tree grow large enough to be used as a cross. Henceforth, it shall be slender and bent and twisted and its blossoms shall be in the form of a cross—two long and two short petals. And in the center of the outer edge of each petal there will be nail prints, brown with rust and stained with red, and in the center of the flower will be a crown of thorns, and all who see it will remember.' "

Red mottling appears on the tree's leaves in autumn and has been associated with the Savior's blood on the cross. The pink dogwood is said to be blushing for shame because of the cruel purpose it served on Calvary. The weeping dogwood further symbolizes this sorrow and regret.

Another tree legend concerns the weeping willow. According to the myth, the branches of this tree originally had thorns which were used to make the thorny crown worn by Christ at the Crucifixion. The tree, however, feeling great sorrow over having caused the Savior so much pain, wept and drooped, and its sharp thorns changed themselves into soft, sad-colored leaves so that they would never again cause any suffering.

Of all the flowers which bloom at Easter time, the passionflower contains the most detailed structural relationship to the tools of the crucifixion. Its ten petals, five white and five purple, symbolize the apostles, excluding Peter, who denied, and Judas, who betrayed Christ. The circle of small, violet-tipped filaments is symbolic of the crown of thorns. The three stigmata rising from a column in the center of the flower represent the nails which were used to secure Christ to the cross. Below the stigmata is the style, which represents the sponge used to moisten the Savior's lips. The five stamens, protruding from the style are suggestive of the five wounds. A coiling tendril which shoots off from the stem represents the lash used in Christ's beating. Radiating filaments surrounding the crown of thorns suggest the hands of those who scourged him. The flower's leaves, with their three distinct points, symbolize the Holy Trinity. It is not difficult to see why the early Christian missionaries to South America saw so many symbols of the crucifixion within this curiously constructed flower.

The beautiful wild daffodil, another flower synonymous with springtime and Easter, is also the focal point of legend concerning the Passion of Christ. According to fable, this lovely flower first appeared on the night of the Last Supper, blooming especially for our Lord in the Garden of Gethsemane to comfort him in his time of great sorrow. The shape of the flower's corona supposedly resembles the cup or chalice used by our Lord at the Last Supper to hold the sacramental wine. Since some species of these favorite springtime flowers are native to the Holy Land, our Lord more than likely admired their golden beauty and included them as one of the "lilies of the field."

The legends surrounding the colorful blossoming plants and flowers of Easter are as enchanting as the season itself. Man has found within nature symbols of rebirth and renewal, viewing the beauty of springtime as a reflection of the joy embodied in the risen Christ.

Michele Arrieh

The Coming of Spring

Lady Spring has now arrived
With banners flying high.
Tulips nod their colored heads
Under a clear blue sky.

Flowering almonds are in bloom;
Their buds, a lovely pink.
The grass is growing greener
After a fairly recent drink.

Lilac bushes sport new life
And soon will show to all
Their fragrant clustered flowers
On leafy branches tall.

New blooms and blossoms are reflected
On a sky-blue lake.
How lovely are the painted scenes
Which Spring leaves in her wake!

All the world seems gayer
Since new life came to town.
A bit of heaven has arrived
In a lovely springtime gown.

Annette Marquardt

Opulence

April's riches—boundless now—
Spread their magic on the bough;
Pearly buds on trees unfold;
Jonquils wave their wands of gold;
Painted tulips in a row
Kiss the passing winds that blow;
The crocus in resplendent dress
Tint the ground with loveliness;
And the hyacinth's fresh bloom
Wafts a delicate perfume.
After winter's bleak and cold
This is wealth the heart can hold.

F. J. Worrall

Easter Time

Springtime camped in the valley today,
In tents of tall-tree green;
With lupine blues and poppy golds
Spread out as a rug between.

She has nudged the frogs in the still-cool pond;
She has whistled the robin home;
She has brushed the grass with beams from the sun
And used the wind for a comb.

She has washed the face of the hillside rocks
With a quick, hard spatter of rain;
She has kissed the buds on the apple tree,
And blessed the fields of grain.

Yes, Springtime camped in the valley today
And banished the frost's white rime.
But best of all for the waiting world
She has brought us Easter time.

Enola Chamberlin

Let Them Have April

Faith is the promise
Of something unseen,
As winter-hearts yearn
For patches of green.

Paint for those dear hearts
A morning in spring.
Make it a vibrant,
Mysterious thing.

Cover the background
With valley and glen;
Top with a mountain
Where snowcaps have been.

Sketch in a cottage
With tall birches minding—
Mailbox, picket fence,
Country road winding.

Give it distinction,
Sunrise through mist.
Add just a whisper
Of pine trees, dew kissed.

Dimple the brooklet
With ice filagree.
Scatter some violets
To purple the lea.

Freshen drab hollows
With cool, fragrant rain.
Dress all the fruit trees
In blossoms again.

Show them that God
Still walks through the lands.
Let them have April
To hold in their hands.

Alice Leedy Mason

Easter Bouquet

June Masters Bacher

I've gathered fragrant bunches
  Of brilliant Easter bloom,
Reminders of the springtime
  And brevity of gloom.

      The colorful arrangement
        Will light-touch each dark day,
        Keeping friendships safe and warm,
        My cashmere-like bouquet.

Each day I'll share a petal,
  A kindly thought or deed,
Wafting love's aroma to
  Some lonely friend in need.

      Now, if I share my flowers
        It is true they'll fade away.
      But I've kept a bit of Easter
        By giving it away.

Margaret Rorke

Margaret Rorke has spent her lifetime in Saginaw, Michigan, as an attorney, wife, and mother. Like the true Michigander she is, she traveled downstate to earn her Bachelor of Arts and Doctor of Law degrees at the University of Michigan. In addition to being a member of the Michigan Bar, she belongs to the First Congregational Church, P.E.O., Alpha Chi Omega, Woman's National Farm and Garden Association, and served two terms as president of the Saginaw Zonta Club. Mrs. Rorke wrote verse for the *Saginaw News* editorial page for twenty-two years, and her poems have made numerous appearances with Judd Arnett of the *Detroit Free Press,* as well as in women's magazines and trade journals. Her collections of verse include *My Ego Trip,* published in 1976, and *A Cup of Sun,* which was recently completed. The poetry of Margaret Rorke first appeared in Ideals twenty-five years ago and continues to find its place among the writings of our favorite poets.

Thirty Pieces

Oh, what did thirty pieces buy?
They bought the cry of "Crucify."
The profit from a kiss.
They bought a trial that mocked its name.
They bought each false and fear-filled claim
And Pilate's cowardice.

Those bits of silver bought the nails,
The cross, the crown, the human wails,
The vinegar and gall.
They bought release for one who killed
So blood untainted might be spilled . . .
They bought it all.

Those little coins bought death for two,
Our Lord and him who was untrue.
They were a princely price.
They bought for a repenting thief
Whose dying gasp was of belief,
A life in paradise.

They bought the veil that darkened day.
They bought the empty tomb's dismay
And Christianity.
Oh, what are thirty pieces worth?
The shame and glory of the earth
For all eternity.

"He Is Not Here"

"He is not here," the angel said,
For He has risen from the dead.
Tell those who hold him dear.
The heavy stone is rolled away
On this, the world's first Easter Day.
Tell them, "He is not here!"

The Marys told His faithful band,
And soon there spread across the land
The words that conquered fear,
The words that gave a lasting breath
To dim the doubts and dread of death,
The words "He is not here."

The waxen lily's throat proclaims
The glory of the name of names,
The message for our sphere.
The earth repeats with every tongue
What ages since have ever sung,
"Praise God, He is not here."

Let us today with faith renewed
Be Easter-minded and imbued
With great and wondrous cheer.
The risen Lord—the empty grave—
Should cause the ones He came to save
To shout, "He is not here!"

Springtime Prayer

Oh, Lord of Spring in soil and air,
Grant me a life more full and fair
By putting springtime there.

Grant me a mind that opens up
Like petals of the buttercup
To see, to sense, to sup.

In me put power to push and grow
Unhampered by the cold and snow—
Past winter's wind and woe.

Give me a heart by spring renewed
And fed till fertile with the food
Of love and gratitude.

Implant my soul with strength of seed
That works with wisdom against the weed
To fill some human need.

Please oil my every spoken word
With what You use to "song" the bird
So I'll be sweeter heard.

Oh, Lord, to balance what is rife
With self-concern and senseless strife
Put springtime in my life.

A Cup of Sun

An old cracked cup sat on the stair,
For I forgot and left it there.
A shaft of sunlight filled its bowl
And warmed what would have been a hole.

How much like me—that old cracked cup—
Made happy by what fills it up.
For me, it's warmth that comes from love
And rays of faith from up above.

Intangible these fillers be:
The cup's full glow, the midst of me;
And, yet, when all is said and done,
Life's finest is its cup of sun.

Let Me See

Let me see something lovely,
Oh, Lord, let me see
All the beauty and magic
And wonders there be!
Let me watch trees a-budding
And birds on the wing.
Let me listen to crickets
And hear streamlets sing.

Let me view every mountain
With awe that it's due.
Let me feel every flower's
A mirror of You.
In the springtime and summer,
In winter and fall,
Let me sense that each season
Has meaning for all.

Open vistas to pastures
Where pictures are real.
Sun and stars, sea and sky,
Let me know their appeal.
Let me see something lovely,
Oh, Lord, let me see
That it's all here for seeing,
But that's up to me.

Whose Garden?

I own a garden.
I plant and I hoe,
But I've a partner
I think you might know.
He mixes the seasons
And ripens my seeds.
For His own reasons
He adds a few weeds.
He gives me sunshine
And showers and soil,
Sparks my ambition
And ardor to toil,
Smiles at my pride in
The things I have grown
And when I speak of
The garden "I" own.

Secret Information

Mary Lou Yuckert

Would you like to know a secret?
Well, I'll tell you one I know:
The Easter Bunny's coming.
My mama told me so.

He'll bring a basket filled with eggs
And leave it in my yard,
And I will find it Easter morn,
If I look very hard.

I shouldn't tell my secret,
But I think it should be shared.
You ought to know that Bunny's coming,
So you can be prepared!

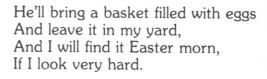

North Woods Notebook
Colored Eggs and Jelly Beans

My husband, Bob, was the youngest of ten children born to Comb and Anna Andersen Bourgeois. The family lived in Park Falls, Wisconsin, when Bob was born on August 20, 1923; during his childhood there were several moves to farms and small towns throughout northern Wisconsin.

Bob's memories of his childhood remain vivid. When he talks about those distant days, the memories come alive; they are echoes of a way of life that has all but disappeared from the American scene.

Bea Bourgeois

In northern Wisconsin, it's still very cold in March and early April; by the time Easter rolled around, we were all pretty sick and tired of winter. But I think my Mother was more anxious for spring than any of us.

Every year, right around Easter, Ma would try to force apple blossoms to bloom. It was almost as though she was trying to force spring to come. She would bring in small branches from some of the trees in our orchard and pound the ends with a hammer. She'd rest them carefully in a vase of water, and then she'd wait and hope. Sometimes it worked, and sometimes it didn't.

If Easter fell late enough in April, Ma would go out in the woods to look for trailing arbutus. Once in awhile she'd spot some, blossoming under the snow. I still remember that sweet fragrance coming from the Easter basket centerpiece on the dining room table.

My brothers Ed and Milt and I could hardly wait until noon on Holy Saturday, and I think we began to eat nonstop when the clock struck twelve. After giving up candy for those forty Lenten days, we were dying for the taste of something sweet!

Some of my older brothers and sisters had married and left home, and others were working in Ashland or Washburn. It was fun to have everybody back home for Easter dinner—our first reunion since Christmas. Ma and the girls always turned out a feast—sometimes roast chicken, a special treat in those days, or maybe a venison roast that came from the deer Pa had hunted the previous fall. Ma served her homemade chokecherry jelly and all kinds of home-canned pickles and relishes— even pickled eggs in beet juice. We had an Easter cake for dessert, which Ma decorated to look like a rabbit by snipping marshmallows for the ears and nose.

As poor as we were, Ma always produced Easter baskets full of treats for the children. She would make the "baskets" out of Mother's Oats boxes and cover them with yellow or green construction paper. There was no such thing as colored plastic grass, so Ma used a handful of hay as a nest for our candy and cookies.

She made fudge and divinity, and we each got some maple sugar candy that the Indians in the settlement had made. Ma baked sugar cookies in chicken and rabbit shapes, too, but the biggest surprise was always "boughten" jelly beans, which I still love, and those brightly colored candy eggs with soft marshmallow centers.

If we happened to have brown eggs (those were no good for coloring), we'd trade them with the Indians for some white ones. We used food coloring and onion skins, and once in awhile Ma and Dad would buy packaged dyes to color the eggs.

Each basket had some of those furry little yellow chicks nestled in it, too, and I used to get upset if the chicken happened to stick to one of my pieces of candy. We each got one of those delicate pastel papier mache rabbits or chickens that came from the dime store in town. I loved them because they had a pocket that was filled with jelly beans, and when I had eaten all the candy I kept them on top of my dresser for decoration. Now they're collector's items!

As a child, I really believed the Easter Bunny worked late at night to get our baskets ready and then hide them in the strangest places around the house. One year I found mine in Ma's washing machine, and I thought that Bunny was pretty clever.

We had a lot of good times hunting for colored eggs, too. Some of them were in the usual places—behind the flour sack in the pantry, or under the couch in the living room. I remember one year when Milt and I were tearing through the house on our hunt, and we discovered a beautiful purple egg in the drawer of Ma's old foot-treadle sewing machine, behind the spools of thread and the bobbins.

There was no such thing as an "Easter Parade" when I was growing up. First of all, it was much too cold for light spring clothing; we wore our heavy winter jackets to church. And secondly, nobody ever got new clothes just because it was Easter. My sister Agnes remembers that the girls in the family got new dresses three times a year: when school started, at Christmas, and when school ended.

Because I was the youngest, I had to wear everybody else's hand-me-downs. If Ted, Frank, Ed, and Milt were done with it, I inherited it. I used to look through the Montgomery Ward catalog and wonder what it would be like to have a brand new suit that had never belonged to anyone else!

When we "paraded" to church on Easter Sunday, I would inevitably be wearing a pair of Milt's pants and a coat that had belonged to Ed—tailored over to fit me, of course, but a "Secondhand Rose" just the same.

EASTER GREETING

Easter Is . . .

Easter is a reminding time . . .
 Of colored eggs and pretty dresses,
  Of yellow chicks and curly tresses.

Easter is a renewing time . . .
 For baby bunnies, birds, and bees,
  For sun and rain on growing trees.

Easter is a grateful time . . .
 For all our blessings every day,
  For health and friends along the way.

Easter is a believing time . . .
 That Christ arose for us to see
  The way to grow eternally.

Easter is a joyful time . . .
 For thoughts, for growth, for songs to sing.
 Yes, Easter is a constant spring.

Ruth Carrington

Easter Greeting

Kittens cradled in my arms
Are like a bright bouquet;
Little ears like petal tips
Make colorful array.

Kitten Bouquet
Eva N. Ehrman

Each little fluffy head seems like
A pansy with eyes and a nose,
Yet little feet with stickery claws
Are more like thorns on a rose.

I love to hold them all at once,
This bouquet sweet and new.
The difference is they really talk—
These flowers purr and mew!

A Country Lane in Spring

Carice Williams

To wander down a country lane
Some quiet day in spring
And see the earth awake and stir
Surpasses anything.

What happy, poignant memories
Reach out this April day,
As apple blossoms, pink and white,
Put on their best display.

The soft caress of April's breeze,
The quiet springtime rain,
Bring cheer and inward peace as I
Stroll down a country lane.

The murmurings of the little brook,
The songs of birds so dear,
All whisper to me as I pass
That God is very near.

In a Gentle Month of Spring

Beverly J. Anderson

Let me walk a country roadway
In a gentle month of spring,
When the dogwood trees are blooming
And the birds are on the wing.

Let me walk through rainbow meadows
Where the gala blossoms sway
To the symphonies of wind-song
In a lovely spring ballet.

Let me seek shade-dappled pathways
Where the honeysuckle twine;
Where the squirrels play neath lace plum trees
And earth's pulse is tuned with mine;

For nothing's quite so thrilling,
Can so make my spirit sing,
As following nature's footsteps
In a gentle month of spring.

The Breads of Easter
Darlene Kronschnabel

A delectable part of springtime and Easter is fragrant, sweet, yeast bread. The breads of Easter are a special part of our heritage. Their fragrance filled country kitchens for generations, promising an end to austere Lenten fasting.

The hot cross bun is perhaps the most popular Easter recipe. It probably originated in pre-Christian England, where the bun was baked in honor of the Anglo-Saxon goddess, Eastre, on her spring name day. Then, with the rise of Christianity, the custom of serving the fragrant, spicy buns transferred from these pagan beginnings to Easter.

Easter breads traditionally are baked in various shapes. Some of the sweet yeast breads or cakes, spicy-rich and fruit-laden, come to us at Easter baked in a circle to symbolize eternity. Some are braided, whereas others are buns. The Russian kulich is baked in a tall cylindrical loaf form, and the Greek-inspired anise loaf displays a whole egg.

Borrow some of these breads from other lands for traditional Easter feasting or just delicious springtime eating, for the breads of Easter, flavorful and tasty fresh, are welcome whenever you bake. Such are the simple pleasures of life.

ANISE LOAF

1 pkg. dry yeast
¼ c. water
½ c. milk, scalded
⅓ c. sugar
¼ c. butter
½ t. salt
¼ t. oil of anise
6 drops oil of cinnamon
2¾ to 3 c. flour
1 egg
1 egg in shell, uncooked, tinted red
1 egg, slightly beaten
1 T. water
2 T. sesame seed

Soften dry yeast in warm water and set aside. Pour scalded milk over sugar, butter and salt, stirring until butter melts. Cool to lukewarm. Stir in flavorings. Add 1 cup of the flour; mix well. Stir in 1 egg and softened yeast; beat well. Add remaining flour or enough to make a soft dough. Turn out on lightly floured surface. Cover and let rest 10 minutes. Knead until smooth and elastic. Place in lightly greased bowl, turning once to grease surface. Cover; let rise in warm place until double. Punch down. Let rise again until almost double. Turn out on lightly floured surface and divide dough in thirds. Form in balls. Cover and let rest 10 minutes. Using your hands, roll each part to form a strand 16" long, tapering ends. Line up strands 1" apart on greased baking sheet. Braid loosely without stretching dough, beginning in middle and working toward either end. Pinch ends together. Tuck tinted uncooked egg, large end up, in center of braid. Cover and let rise until almost double, about 40 minutes. Combine beaten egg and water; brush over braid; sprinkle with sesame seed. Bake in 375° oven about 25 minutes or until golden.

HOT CROSS BUNS

2 c. milk, scalded
1 c. butter
1 c. sugar
2 cakes yeast dissolved in ⅓ c. lukewarm water
2 eggs
8 c. flour
1 t. salt
1½ c. raisins
1 t. cinnamon or nutmeg

Pour scalded milk over butter and sugar, stirring to dissolve. Cool to lukewarm. Add the yeast mixture and eggs. Mix well. Gradually add the flour and salt, reserving a small amount of flour to dust raisins. Add spice and floured raisins to the dough and knead in thoroughly. Place in a buttered bowl, cover, and let rise until doubled. Punch the dough down and turn it out onto a floured board. Shape dough into 30 buns and place on buttered cookie sheets. Cover and let rise for 30 minutes, then very carefully press the shape of a cross into each bun, using a spatula or the back of a knife. Bake in a 375° oven for 10 minutes. Reduce heat to 350° and continue baking until buns are browned, about 10 to 15 minutes longer. Frost either the entire bun or just the shape of the cross.

WHITE FROSTING

1 egg white
1 t. lemon juice, vanilla or almond extract
Confectioners' sugar

Beat egg white until stiff, adding confectioners' sugar gradually until mixture is thick. Add flavoring. If frosting is too thin, add more confectioners' sugar.

Wild Goose Lagoon

It happened one spring Sunday morning toward the end of May that I came upon a family gathering near a lagoon in one of our local parks. The air was mild, predicting what was to come in June. Cool breezes from the northwest, however, reminded me of those long days of March and April when winter did not want to relinquish its grip.

There they were, on the first family picnic of their lives, a pair of Canada geese and four recently hatched goslings. Many of the species flew to distant territories hundreds of miles north, where Canadian provinces became a place to raise their young. For generations v-shaped flocks had made the northward journey each spring, only to return when the leaves of autumn were in brilliant display. But by fate, instinct, or some other unexplained phenomenon, this pair of geese had decided on a ten-acre parcel of land in the heart of a busy residential and industrial section of Milwaukee's southwest side.

That one day in May brought me back to the lagoon for several more weeks, eight to be exact. The relationships among the members of the goose family intensified during that time. Now there was time for matters beyond basic survival. Forms of recreation such as swimming and sunning themselves were frequent family activities. When the young goslings investigated new and unfamiliar areas, the watchful elder geese never let innocent situations become dangerous.

I guess I was not the only person to enjoy and learn something from those days in the park. On several of my weekly jaunts, other interested park users stopped to chat and communicate their admiration for those special visitors. One elderly man remarked that the beauty and the peace of the scene before us rivaled many similar scenes in the northern part of the state. Another occasion brought a gray-haired grandmother and her two-year-old grandson to share with the geese pieces of bread carried from home in a plastic bag. Even an occasional jogger broke stride to admire the goose family, without concern for the time on the stopwatch or the distance measured on the pedometer.

Eight weeks passed, and I began to notice changes taking place. The goslings acted more confident, and their feathers indicated that a further change was imminent. Along with the dark brown color that replaced the last streaks of light yellow, a fuller pair of wings gave proof that someday soon the young geese would spread their wings and set out in their own direction.

The hours spent visiting the geese and their admirers taught me much about sitting, looking and listening. In the current age of uncertainty, when news from around the world affects us whether we like it or not, taking time to appreciate the very simple things in nature so close to home truly was a rewarding change of pace.

Here it was, right before me, the "natural high" of the sights, sounds, and the colors of creation, those inalienable rights that Aldo Leopold, a famous naturalist, once wrote about in his *Sand County Almanac*. Leopold had an eye for those attractive simple things when he wrote, "like winds and sunsets, wild things were taken for granted until progress began to do away with them. Now we face the question whether a still higher 'standard of living' is worth its cost in things natural, wild, and free. For us of the minority, the opportunity to see geese is more important than television, and the chance to find a pasque-flower is a right as inalienable as free speech."

This communication among living creatures, different yet alike, human and nonhuman, in "wild goose lagoon," so close to my home, was created strictly from chance. As I sat on the park bench enjoying the peacefulness of the day, I thought about similar opportunities in our environment that often go unnoticed. Hopefully, more of us will develop an awareness and take the time to discover other such things "wild, natural, and free."

Gregg Trojanowski

The Magic World of Springtime

The magic world of springtime
Is at our door again,
With smiling skies and warming breeze
And gentle April rain.
The gladsome songs at dawning
Of small birds in a tree
Are telling us that springtime joys
Are bursting constantly.

The magic world of springtime
Has laid her bounteous store
Of flowers and trees and singing birds
Outside our very door.
The hills are carpeted in green,
And soft blue are the skies.
A magic world has come to life
Before our very eyes.

Carice Williams

The Passing of Time

Everything put on this earth gives up its youth and takes on the look of age. The young twig gives way to the mighty tree, each spring unveiling new branches to add to its grandeur.

Each great ocean beats against magnificent rocky shores until nothing is left but small sandstones and eroded crevices, enlarging its vastness with each new year.

All the birds of the sky and the animals that walk the land must surrender to the passing of time. And, as we grow old and new life is born, we must remember that we are only nearing the end of one existence and embarking upon a new one, just as we did the hour of our birth.

No one escapes time. And when our years have been many and our days are numbered, we must be patient with the exuberance of youth, show understanding to those things that are different, accept what is new and try to remember that "old," does not mean "useless," for when we enter heaven, we will be the young, and the elders of that time will be just as strange to us as we are now to our youth.

Easter Message

The Easter bells peal out their chimes
  Of glorious good cheer.
They bring good tidings, tell the world
  The message of the year.

They tell of Jesus Christ, our Lord,
  Who gave His life for us
And who was resurrected—news
  So great and glorious.

The Easter message! Happy song!
  All Christians must declare
Their praise of Christ the risen Lord,
  And all His love must share.

                              Roy Z. Kemp

ACKNOWLEDGMENTS

MARCH SYMPHONY by May Allread Baker. From THE GIFT OF THE YEAR by May Allread Baker. Copyright © 1964 by The Brethren Press, Elgin, Illinois. Used by permission. THE TIME OF THE TRILLIUMS by Colleen Reece. Previously published in THE RURAL-ITE, May 1977. Our sincere thanks to the following author whose address we were unable to locate: L. D. Stearns for TRIUMPH.

COLOR ART AND PHOTO CREDITS
(in order of appearance)

Front and back covers, Colour Library International (USA) Limited; inside front and back covers, Gerald Koser; Pink blossom, Fred Sieb; Garden splendor, Fred Sieb; Spring tulips, Fred Sieb; "Woodland Flowers", Trilliums near Valmy, Wisconsin, Ken Dequaine; First flowers, Colour Library International (USA) Limited; Woodland Serenity, Gerald Koser; Springtime on Apache Trail, Arizona, Ed Cooper; 1970 Oberammergau Passion Play, German National Tourist Office; 1970 Passion Play Street Scene, Germany, Josef Muench; Passion flower, Fred Sieb; THE LAST SUPPER, Gustav Wegener, Three Lions, Inc.; THE SLEEPING DISCIPLES, Gustav Wegener, Three Lions, Inc.; CHRIST IN BONDAGE, G. Raadsig, Three Lions, Inc.; Stained-glass window, H. Armstrong Roberts; Lilies, Fred Sieb; Formal garden, H. Armstrong Roberts; Tulip bouquets, Four By Five, Inc.; Easter surprise, H. Armstrong Roberts; Easter favorites, Fred Sieb; Cuddly kittens, Pat Powers; Farmstead near Pownal, Vermont, Fred Sieb; CANADA GOOSE AND GOSLINGS, Sharon Manka, Gerald Koser; Washington tulip farm near Mt. Vernon, Ed Cooper; Birch haven, Fred Sieb; Peaceful chapel, Fred Sieb.

For Mother . . .

Mother's Day Ideals lovingly portrays the special feelings a mother and child share in beautiful color photography and delightful, heartwarming articles.

You will marvel at the breathtaking beauty of sculpture by Cybis Porcelain. Learn of the craftsmanship which creates intricate designs in beaded fashions. Take a leisurely stroll through fragrant springtime gardens. Read of the many attributes of motherhood through the writings of Carice Williams, our featured poet.

Enjoy the world of Ideals today and everyday of the year with a subscription for yourself and your family. Remember Mom, your mother-in-law or a close friend with a gift subscription that will bring many hours of reading pleasure . . . let Ideals say "I'm thinking of you" year round!